THE
DJINN'S SIN

THE DJINN'S SIN

SAXTON

Library of Congress Control Number: 2023914885

ISBN: 978-1-960093-78-3   (Paperback)
ISBN: 978-1-960093-79-0   (eBook)

Printed in the United States of America

———

Dedicated to the most beautiful,
Soulfully resound flower,
That doth bloom,
In the garden of Humanity.
May the waters nurture you,
Upon journeys of growth.

———

Circles

In roundabout,
No escape,
Stuck in place,
Ball and Chain,
Held down my grace.
Gravity, heavy is its weight,
Locked down to stay,
Swallowing the damn key.
So temporary, its not forever,
Just time amidst material plains,
Uneternal reigns, biding rage,
In realms of a mortal constant.
An exchange of bridging trades,
Between the suns and the rains,
Where there is growth,
The confinement of the circle breaks.

Empty Woods

The winds carry,
Lost words long forgotten,
Burdened, by the empty woods.
Chasing an understanding,
Its' whirlwinds passing through,
Leaving the branches rattled,
Leaves all shaken,
And trees warped in their dancing.

Control Room

Room of buttons,
Insecure of the unknown,
Piloting a body,
In wake of destruction.
To imprison the choices,
And feelings of others.

The Control Freak,
In the panel of the mind,
Leaving you with doubt,
And unanswered questions,
Manipulating, and mutilating,
Your own perceptions.

A small gift of insanity,
Taking the power of self,
Robbing you of all emotions,
The finale, a theft of voice,
Quieted down without much a choice.
In keep of rewritten events,
Both of truth,
And factual evidences.

—

Temperance, and patience,
Are the bones of strong mind,
And kindness, a kind of water,
Bringing vitality alive.

—

Depravity

Bland and boring are the muddied shallows!
Stirred, but not deep at all,
Not able to handle, or hold space,
For the darkness of the shadow.
The trees have all rotted hollow,
In doomly bloom of gloom.
Withered lands tilled of sorrow,
The frown of flowers,
Death of lands.

Of Natural Wonder

How beautiful are the,
~~Stars and Clouds~~,
Oh, wait!
I meant satellites and smog,
Something, seems a bit off.
Something is definitely wrong,
The city lights' hiding,
A most cherished sight,
Existing upon organic life,
Up above your head,
In the sleepy night.

Ah, but the religion of science, right?

Ecological Succesion

Stuck in a room,
Emotionally, a lasting,
Survival cage match,
No hand raised, or hit back.
Object of wrathful rage,
To pieces, with anger and hate.
Without apologies or forgiveness,
Left upon indulgences,
No affection,
The affliction,
Much like an infection,
Untreated rejection.
No mole in the walls,
Just misdirected fists,
Harm of self,
Stabbing goddamned,
Mattresses,
Hurting yourself,
Or the world,
But painfully the years change,
Clinging to the pasts sway,
A headache you can't medicate.
Explosive fireball.
Bending the world,
To your very whims,

and thoughts on reality.
Mentally broken down,
The sodden,
Sob of pathetic rivers.
Burdening another hurt,
A vessel to heal,
Animal without fear.
Vested the jungles,
Of tar and tears,
Prickly needles and brushes,
The searing heat,
The cold foreboding freeze,
All that we cannot speak.
Still did not run or leave,
Even past rapidness amphetamine,
Knowing souls so enticingly addicting.
Past it all,
To skin or walls,
Not of something lonely,
But diminishing,
The spirit,
What's it even worth to me?
Once the last bit of forestry,
Burns, ashening the grounds,
A new world, has its space to grow,
In place of what we used to know.

Gynecology

At the gynecologist,
To meet vagina scientists!
Not allowed to tour the backrooms,
I understand, so instead,
To bash in the head of boredom,
I shall write about it.
Questions and curiosity,
'Filabia clittoramia,'
The fisherman's seafaring jewel,
Glistening purity,
For the simplicity,
Of an organ,
Foreign to me,
but respectfully,
Held highly,
And mystically.
Worshipped,
Ahh damn goddess,
Crowned Pearl.

What a quiet office,
~Insert jazz guitar solo,~
Maintaining at best rhyme,
In the oddest of times,
Like fine garnishing,

Of rosemary and thyme.

Fangs

I have fangs,
Pushing out the back,
Of my fucking face.
Broken,
Bleeding,
Rotten teeth.
Anger and pain,
Turning to pure savagery,
I'll fucking kill anything.
So much pain,
I can't fucking think,
Coming from the psycho,
Who broke his bones,
Upon the streets,
A night out,
Bleeding out,
Without thoughts of second doubt.

One miserable fucking 'oww.'
Rip 'em out,
Just rip 'em the fuck out.
Anything to stop,
The wretched aching achey, ache.
Pills, seated pussy upon thy face,
Requiems of financial deposites,

I cannot take a break!
To hell with the taxonomy,
Genus modern pharmacoligate.
Adapted to do,
When it is permitted okay.
Just fix the problem,
ANYWAYS!

Cotter

Cloaked by night,
And tied with rope,
As if medieval times,
Tilling the Earth,
Attendant to crops.
Purging the soils,
To bring upon vegetation,
In yield of the growth,
Be it soul or vegetable,
Deepening the truly rooted.
The turning of stones,
Excavations and discovery,
Uncovering personal histories,
To set plot upon a gardeners' archaeology.
All seeds and deeds,
Planted today,
Fruitfully shall bleed,
The bloodshed of physical laborings,
Into the pursuit and budding,
Of new found dreams.

Art?

Symbolically agreed upon,
Esoteric teachings,
Humankind collectively enjoys.
At least what can survive,
And avoids being destroyed.
A stain in time and space,
That makes you feel,
Then think,
A recording so temporal,
Of senses fossailic physical.
How loud does the spirit ring?
In summaries, of an important nothingness,
To the collective festivities of human histories,
Reviving all cultural purposes and liveliness.
Meaning to void,
Teachings entertaining,
Sensual and emotionally,
Regards of conscious captivity.
Last flickers,
For others to dwell,
Accepting change,
To rebel in,
Moments of empathic confession.
Akashic glimpse coincide desire,
Not to aspirations or inspirations pyre,

But fueled upon,
Ones own life force fire.
For imitation is too cheap,
Authentically royal is the real thing,
And such as purity,
Is meant to be.
By slight of will, perceptively,
In death leaving,
Non but feeling.

Saddle Up

With attentiveness,
And quiet ambience,
From depths of the minds,
'Ol willful eye.
Manifestations,
The focus of summonings,
To reality,
From human conscience,
And bounds of the creative prowess.

All of the infinite,
What comes into being.
Intelligence, dreams, realms,
All the instinct,
Guiding ones curiosity.
To the unknown,
Where wisdom is known.

Braving new fronts and experiences,
Just having fun underneath,
Both moon and sun,
Within crevices of confusion.
Pie, slice of life,
Cheers,
To whichever path ye be on.

Saddle up
The journey before dawn.
And judgments be cast far from yuh'.

Unicorn

Withholding an amassed flood of energy,
Within the night of the summers bizarre.
Sales of vendors, and music,
Settling the nights starts.
Racers gather up,
A line of coke starts.
Brewed potions, and herbal wisdoms,
Gather a fantasy fable,
Beyond hours so gentle.
The streets traveled,
And friends abandoned,
Upon sidewalk flowers.
Pleasure powder,
Opened, thus sealed way,
Sensation changes,
In vibrations, adaptations.
Animalistically craving,
A melding touch,
Can't get enough.
Chemical composition,
Rearrangement of positions,
Sacred sanctions,
Revelry of exotic pleasure,
Gems of buried treasure,
Graces, joyous and euphoric.

Ritualistic ecstasy,
Summoned forth,
The taboo, and demons of lust.
Physical mergement combining flesh,
With spiritual surgeance,
As one spirit of sex,
Bodies connect,
In the very servitude of another.
Cosmically explosive,
In orgasmic exchange,
Just a taste,
As we waltz and play,
To shift and recreate,
To a new state of being.
Togetherness tied to fire,
Hotter and hotter,
At peak of climax.
Entangled quivernce,
Enchanted remembrance,
As if discovering a unicorn.
Sexy, sacred,
Magically delicious,
The first time of safety,
In the arms of experience,
Strangely and tenderly,
Special of virgin choice.

The sidewalks to my lips,
And then to the car again.

Accepting breeded lusts,
Kinkly opening up,
To norm defined fetish.
Quainted as love,
Beauty of soul,
And connectivity vibrational.
A surprise to just be,
Something transitioning.

Although,
I'm not asking questions.
Just ripping of any fibers of clothes,
Getting naked and sexual.

Sour Candy

Can you taste the electricity,
Nitric acids,
A taste in symphony.
Hurting my cavities,
Taste gourmet,
Eclecticity of batteries.
Soulful novelties,
Glucatical masterpiece,
Flavorful mystery,
Leaving more,
To hunger.

Nocturnes

Night Owls,
The city ashut sleeps,
Go on, perch, and sing.
No rush where to be,
As the city slowly sleeps.
Just thoughts of clarity,
Watching through the nightfall.
Keepers of time,
In the delight of silence,
And absence of sunlight,
Prey upon the idle prize.

Beyond Reaches

Beings of energy,
Seemingly change everything,
In all that is studied,
Leaders alienated in history,
Guiding those in longing,
Born upon infernal sufferings,
Of eternal modernistic evolving.
The rejected modernistic of society,
Giving culture and notoriety,
Of one hungry underground belly.
`Toxicity may be of genuine nature,
Verses the manipulated projection,
Of human nature.
All is left to vote on stature,
But before you'll run some tests,
and practice killing and misunderstanding,
each other.

Born Earth

Built from the very Earths,
And all its preciousness,
The stubborn and the sturdy.
From irons welled deep of cores,
Not of pretentious finical ores.
More'er ancients deep in woods,
Or of elopes mountainous,
and keeps for goods.
Born of Earth in solid form,
Species, homosapien,
Another animal inhabiting,
The ecosystematics recorded,
Finically habitualabit.
A tragic, yet unbalanced,
Occurence,
Unborn to the servitude,
of anothers adherence.

We aren't
'Workers or Slaves.'

Venom

Hut of darkness,
Upon a new den,
Jungle hidden,
Of streams and concrete,
The dirt you breathe.
Eyes in crouch,
Sixth sense watching about,
The one in detection,
Of frequence.
A snake moves about,
Slithering around,
It's hunting grounds.
All is prey,
It may take more than a day.
Allegiance paves way,
Upon the venoms,
Medicine is made.

Hatchette

Marked as enemy,
Brutalized without mercy,
Relentlessly with full suffering.
From satellite view,
To wildernesses out of view,
A demon haunting you.
The icing of sweet revenge,
Waters have boiled.
Just know you shouldn't of started shit,
Wannabe jugglish hatchet bitch!
Stay awake and spun,
Muahahaha,
I'm just having some fun.
Feel the nightmare of despair,
As you are awake,
And I am there.
Running away,
To where?
Should of killed me,
And split my skull,
When you had me in the air.
Instead of running into hiding,
From beyond sightly blindings.

Paragons

No symbolic paragon,
Before or after,
Can gift,
What must be achieved,
Through hands of,
Solitary means.
For you are,
To YOUR own being,
Not defined,
By ideas projected,
Through chants,
Of other peoples meaning.
Life embraced,
Lived fully,
By you.

—

Tyrannosaur

Teanie, tiny, meanie,
Belchianic and beastly,
Roars most mighty,
Viscous at chomp,
Biting upon your heinie.
Playfully carnivorous,
Driven mad hangry,
Screeching ungodly!
To feed a
Tyrannosaurus baby.

The Seattle Pepper

Half a moon,
A Twosome divulges,
Upon the midnights roads.
Money broke,
But the gas tank is full,
Taking to shadows.
The ocean, rivers, and lands,
Bridged together miles up,
The grand narrow dusky isle.
Foggy vines from the trees,
Entangling all that I can see.

'Wait. Stop the car, I have to pee.'
Zips
Quietly as the city sleeps,
The outsiders take to the mists.

The sky path opening up,
The guide to our destination,
Stars of a mysterious location.
Pirates cove, we leave the ship,
To traverse beyond anchored landings.
Wandering far out to stone our standings,
And feast upon packed lunch,
Under the sting of the melting sun.

Baked basking,
Restfully in passing,
Guardian of naps and dreams,
Before the visiting,
Synagogues of music.
Spicy is patience,
Amidst the heat of parking,
The tease finally started biting,
To visit a dancing chili pepper,
The quests in quests start their lining.
Concessions of a journeys plot,
Revitalizing reasonable starts,
Leaving ears bloodshot.

Jammed traffic stops,
The night ends in the park,
A comatose to gather energy.
By the end of gallantries,
And escape from the city,
Released back into the country.
Unhinged road trips,
And on to the next.

Tombed

To all that dies before speech,
Left only bitterly,
The strongest of all feelings,
The unspoken harborings.
The tomb forever,
Remains sealed,
The chance is gone,
All is lost,
And to the winds,
Crumble into dusts.
What point satisfies enough?
Keeling over and giving up.
Non but questions and blood gush,
An anxious mess giving of human rust.
If valued, sacred or special,
Then cast about,
'Ol Spellion,
May it be known.
Voice is not long gone,
Just the kindles of passion.

Cyliclist

Stressed, depressed,
Exhausted, ignored,
Overworked, unbalanced,
Paranoid, and overloaded.
To pull the odds of favor,
Into a universal blessing.
In prayer of what's meant to be,
The equivocally of understanding,
Matured reciprocity of nurturing,
Not another source of negativity.
My eyes do bleed,
Body moves without sleep,
Went from days to a week.
Stopped learning,
Couldn't seek,
Trapped to cylicl maintenance,
Catering survival and angst,
Shackled to dictation.
Watching as myself slip,
Further and further,
From any identity.
Not what I used to be,
And hate the spirits
Counciled in gathering,
Despite the absence of any real bodies.

Complacent

A gin of silence,
Dissociations creeping through,
Heartbroken avenue.
Midlife crisis,
Self induced,
Mental breakdown.
At soul frown,
From a goofy clown.
Handling up,
When no one is around.
Wandering through town,
And as usual,
Not one sound.

But it's cool,
The rain keeps,
The flames and embers,
From burning everything away.

Hydration

Go on ye' 'ol,
Young traveler.
Drink of the waters,
And rejoin its' flow.
Everlasting,
Eternal.

The Orange Times

The crispining has begun,
The season of orange,
Oven coaled forest,
Burning with desires,
Shroud of people.
Covenant to summers harvest,
Things apple, pumpkin and cinnamon,
Embrace and acceptance,
The world,
A constant state of change.
And being,
Something close,
and simpler to meaning.

Gifts of Gaia

For every tear wept,
All poured of bloodshed.
A blade of grass,
Or flower grew instead.
To the place at which Gaia,
Remains at rest.
To her, your strength,
In bloom, a gift so natural,
And precious.

Cozy Pause

Sleepy coffee snuggles,
Warm blanket blossoms,
Holding flames closely.
A pause in life,
A brief moment,
Where all feels alright.
Take the day to rejuvenate,
And trust, of peace and hope,
Not just now,
But in practice,
It follows,
Oozing out,
The way love,
Flows.

Jealousy

Endless and powerless,
Another dead end.
Falling exhausted,
Bleeding again,
Refusal to change.
That's okay,
What equates exchange?
Sacrifice and strife,
Find their way to confide,
The air keeping flames high,
And lies alive.
Another pointless fight,
Inedited from jealousy,
A goddamn disease.

The Rocks

Here it goes again,
Fucked up repetition,
Behavioral patterns,
Of annihilation.
Defensive to illogical nonsense,
The fact is, that's thoughtless.
Can't cry, bitch, or complain,
Another cause of argument,
And point of blame,
Focus shifts a new excuse.
At the floor with shame,
Nothing can be done anyways.
Voice has been gone,
Steeping in a bag of wrong.
And can't choose to hurt,
Where the source of pain fruits,
Diminishing the ripened bloom.
Can't let it poison the root,
Or burden trajectory of mood,
Leaving me mentally confused.
Emotionally in turmoil,
Sanity buried into the soils.
And still going through the trouble,
Digging through all the rubble,
To find the cause of destruction.

Nerves always threatened,
In avoidance of physical unravels,
At survival against fires travels.

Pushed to a point I must choose.
To have to forcefully eject,
From negligence and disrespect,
And just be through.
Forward to move,
Alone, without you.
More pride than to keep begging thee,
To always be upset with myself,
Or generally pissing disdain angrily.
Day after day to keep in repeat,
Petty hurts, the stress,
At soul so unhealthy.

It isn't worth the pain,
To have your sense of self,
Stripped and taken away.
To not feel or think anything,
Except projections of another being.
To worry about repercussions,
From even existing,
Breathing, and blinking.
Can't make decisions,
Have happy meanings.

Written all before,

Same lines and rhymes,
Maybe abiding time,
Before shit blows up,
Out of line.
Can't try to keep fixing,
Building, or bridging,
Something breaking itself.

All the strengths of feelings,
Of love,
Cannot help but,
To sink with the ship.
To have tried, and cried,
Watching it all die.

—

With such,
Heaviness,
A wounded animal,
Walks around town,
Bleeding about.

—

Roe v. Wade:
In Concerto Overture no.3

Together in rebellious mass,
Rally the forces in an instance,
To plant a bomb in their office.

Let's use their corpses,
To fertilize new appointments,
Due to their choice,
And the disappointed.
How did such weak men,
Become appointed,
And anointed with power?
Their death comes closer in passing hours.
The vaginaless,
Get no say in it!
Unless willing to be castrated.
Put a hole in the face,
Of the Supreme Court Cabinet,
The ones to truly be aborted.

To create new order,
After revolution and blood shed.
To fight and die,
For our Women.

Deceased

Rotting inside skin and meat,
Creatures delight,
Taking a bite of flesh to eat!
They die of poisonings,
Oh, they thought,
The taste be sweet!
Chew upon the deceased,
In decaying curse,
A dead wild beast!

Vomeronasular

Intuitively off,
Can't shake these vested feelings off.
Head to, toe, a complete bother,
And an anxiousness that keeps to shudder.
Nobody knows,
And so a strange mystery grows,
With answers still unknown.
Trust in the compass of soul,
It's fractalled, shattered, pieces,
Broken up by the world,
Give direction after all.
Hear the whispers of winds,
Speaking its' tongues,
Sit still and listen.
What secret are you harboring?
Spill and share,
To pull wisdom,
From the air.

Mute

Awake to dissociate,
Immovable mute distance,
Silent tears, just ignored.
Not wanting to deal with a chore,
Quieted just as before,
Left to self vices.
Cold, moody, silence,
Known all to well,
A special and personal hell.

The Cloud

The cloud envelopes,
Following me around.
Can't kill this frown,
But can insanely,
Laugh like the clowns.
Gruesome, dark, and stormy,
A brood of mournings.
Blend of the blood and rains,
Endocrines mountainous pains.
All it does,
Is pour until May.
And even then,
Light seems to part ways,
Prismatically.
The same olde ways.
Functionality,
Of deepened sorrows,
Somethings never change.
In place of buried remains.

Blindings

It is of unspoken hidings,
Poisoning the well springs,
From sources we drink.
In disarray of known purity,
The unknown who should be.
For you or me,
The acceptance of identity,
Nutritionally healthy,
For sakes of you and me.
Secrets of silent mystery,
Up to the light, perceptually,
To a vague sense of peace,
Or self experimenting.
To know,
And yet pretend,
Of blindness.

Gasps

Strangely dreams,
Awaking panic,
What does it mean?
What is real,
And what is true,
Finding a branch to cling to.

The Fridge

Locked into the miserable cold,
With machines to disassemble,
And baths of chemicals.
Reflection in the floor,
In the stomach,
And then right out the door.
Cold waters pool,
Rain suit and boots,
Splashes all around you.
Food mountains,
Enshoveled,
Constant waste,
Unrecycled.
A break, to thaw in place,
All of idle time,
And Sacrifice,
For spare change,
The exchange.

Lev

The Heart,
A tempered shield,
Protective armor,
A bit cold, and dulled,
Years worn to edgeless,
Just as the ancient sword.
Everything, so tangibly real,
Down to the touch, and feel.

The Crickets

This band of crickets kickass!
They have the entirety,
Of entomology,
Moshing!
The worlds natural symphony,
Bringing the August heat,
And liveliness beyond the dawn.
Alone in the forest,
To one of its many of songs.
Overbearing the noise spirit,
Of a viral undying city.
By spell of silence quells,
Hushing the human realm,
Retreat to the sources of nature.
Natural resorts,
At which mana,
Is restored.
The audience must be on its way,
Deepest wish to stay,
And celebrate life this day.

Spinge

In practicing immunities,
To foulness in poisonings.
Through the soils,
Rich and well,
Waters drawn,
Make your face swell.
A churn of noxiousness,
Vomits of provocation,
Processed souring,
And venomous.
The warm, grounding sponge,
Absorbs leads and mercury,
Eating of the toxicities.
Filtrations in cleansing.
In purity refreshings,
All health replenishing,
Soulfully regenerating.
And a mind at peace,
Unwinds and starts mending.

Spittoon

One fruit a day,
Picked of choice,
Spittin' out the seeds.
To see a mystery,
Blossom and fruiate,
The marked pathways,
Planted trails,
Past footwork,
And the unknown.
Whatever it is, you choose to take,
Insight of meeting halfway,
Manifesting your own fate.

Exsanguination

At the end of a slow burn,
3rd Degree,
Of nothingness and output.
The seeker returns,
With hands empty again.
Seared by inability,
Undisciplined habitually,
Not pity or blame,
Can't scape a goat to frame.
By the end of the day,
To know it's all by the brains.

Screens

Screens, screens, screens.
Computerize everything,
Goddamnit so distracting.
How entertaining,
Propagated brainwashing.
An advertised grip,
Upon egos of society,
And all that you don't need.
Screens, screens, screens.
Turn off and unplug,
And give yourself a fucking hug.
Tuning in naturalists acoustically,
Signaling to never reach again,
Or invasively breach overtaken,
The reference point frequency.

Unleash it all from your physical being.

—

To do nothing,
Is to be nothing.
And comfort,
Quite the capable killer.
Space exists,
More than to just occupy,
In reverence to life.
Our endless dance,
With time.

—

NPC Dialogue

It's the same bullshit on repeat,
Like everything you hear on radio pop twenty.
NPC conversations, so soulless,
The customer service voice,
Hiding the fact that I'm annoyed.
Within three said sentences.
The next day loads,
To gather the coinage golds,
Emotionally, a vegetable.
Exchanges lacking actual,
Substance or value.
Intellectual tangibility,
Passionate feelings.
Devoid pitifully of meaning,
To falsetto servitudes of reality.
It's the same bullshit on repeat,
Like everything you hear on radio pop twenty.
NPC conversations, so soulless,
The customer service voice,
Hiding the fact that I'm annoyed.
Within three said sentences.
The next day loads,
To gather the coinage golds,
Emotionally, a vegetable.
Exchanges lacking actual,

Substance or value.
Intellectual tangibility,
Passionate feelings.
Devoid pitifully of meaning,
To falsetto servitudes of reality.

The Shitty Poem

All of us are connected by our assholes,
By a most noble of thrones,
Where the world sits,
Lost to ponder.
In privacy becoming gods or something,
In the bowl vomiting like a sick dog incarnating.
Hours,
And hours,
We offer a chunk of our lives,
Dunking an altered sacrifice.

By insufferable powers of spicy,
I throw my clothes off,
To breathe through my skin.
Letting the chill surfacing,
Feel like I'm dying,
I hate shitting.
Never again.

Of Prostitutes and Slaves

The times of prostitutes and slaves,
How we all sell ourselves in in different ways.
A conscious portion of survival.
No joy to pleasurable happenings,
At night at work, rest, or play,
Whichever you decide, it's okay.
The capitalist path paved,
A living sacrifice,
Offering up body and time,
To pay upon taxation,
And to still thrive.

Either way we're still fucked.

Beaned

Metal snows,
Patched up santa claus,
Throwing horns up,
Amongst Red Sea of clones.
If he'd die tonight it wouldn't mattered.

He was right.
The world would keep going on.
Not a damn thing would stop.
A hole would be left in life,
From all of your surroundings,
You, the thing missing, unknowing.
Ionic bonds left incomplete,
Time remaining to fately deplete.
The end of you,
Isn't quite an ending,
Although death consumes.

To think he shot himself.
And the only response,
To go home,
And microwave a frozen burrito.

Only left to sit and wait,
Meditate, and medicate.

The next day,
Still raised beyond,
Nights dark confections.

That tomorrow,
Will still be there,
Wether we are even aware.

Humachine

Machines in movement,
Thinking about thinking,
But never beginning.
Never stopping to do,
Rest or enjoy the view,
Mindfully blank and empty,
Completely thoughtless.
What's to even feel?
Established purpose?
How odd, trying for the perfect unfinished,
Solving the trivial mysteries,
Left to no explanations.

Fuck 'Em

Demented,
Soulless,
Me,
Hope it feels like a hammer being smashed,
Into your goddamned fucking head,
For each fucked thought you had.
Pulsating a hurt in which your brain stemmed.
I want you to suffer,
And let the cancer eat you alive,
Before you fucking die.
Not a single tear to shed,
No remorse, not even a tinge of sad.
In fact, I'm very glad!
Time to celebrate the good news,
To hear that a rapist was found dead.

Murder and thievery,
Can be justified,
But rape will always remain,
As the only true crime.
Let them agonize,
AND BE CURSED!

Mushroom Suplex

Pull the bike over,
For the mushrooms are flexing strong,
And now bits of Johns' mind are gone.
Inconclusive the idea of destination,
But to find the pieces left,
Hidden in new found location.

Preservatory

Modernized to way of life,
A new age,
And new time.
They before, they after,
Animals of the natural world.
Rulers of the ancient kingdoms,
Remnants of natural extinction,
Lasting in mythological distinctions.

Gardens of Sin

Shields of thorns,
A natural fortress,
Reborn and rebuilt,
By some witches.
Villa d'este a new,
Babylon's secret still hiding,
The minds centered Ryōan-Ji.
Personal Eden,
Where we can always eat,
Our forbidden fruits.
Rolling meadows hillside,
Feast on the nights bonfire,
And no other people,
Alive,
In such a quiet moment of the world.

Core of Universal Connectivity

Accessible and nonjudgemental,
Plane of chaotic intellect,
Of peace, abstain of boring.
More to discover in learning,
By wisdom and knowledge yearning,
In faint egregious intriguiments.
Realms of bridged allegiancies,
Friends in wander, wonder of mystery,
In struggle of depositional histories personally.
In seal of small bonds,
An experienced togetherness.
Core of Universal Connectiveness.

Cutting Ties

Be afraid not,
To step into your own power.
Not to claim, or to conquer.
Simply, to just be.
In remembrance,
Passing sequence,
To new found presence.

Innocence before fear;
Slaughter before peace;
Freedom before order;
Silence before the noise;
Secede of thee,
The minds anchors,
Be on your way,
Unfurling the sails.

Stretch of Restlessness

Tiredness pursues,
A voidness irate,
Annoyed berates.
Where of, the earth opened up,
Consuming all noise,
Not one peep of voice.
Not one sound, subservient choice.
Autonomously robotic,
Repeat w/o rest or change.
At constant sacrifice,
The demand that fire brings,
Unhinged at sense of balance.
Stretched out again to nothingness,
Patience and joy thinning.
Been drained and emptied,
Dulled pointless and prideless.
And now,
I'm sleepy.

Link Box

To know,
Without admittance,
Already at point of fear.
Still can't tell me,
Maybe too cowardess,
To have not done anything.
Trust in thinning,
The spiel so empty,
In plain of isolate.
Away from others,
The burden,
Third wheeled mothers.
Too far gone to recover,
Narcissi's perfect companion,
Favorful to distorted projections.
And if betrayed upon difficult days,
For my sake the universe will rip me away.
Been pained to say it might be best to break,
Synchronized as over glorified roommates,
As lovers to plant reasons to stay.
For sake of health,
To teach,
And show the error,
In contribution of,
Destructive habits.

In life to create new ways,
To hold accountability,
In totality of your being.

Ignorance

Honestly,
Shut the fuck up,
For just a goddamn second.
Like when we obey the,
Silences, we long for in nature.
If you listen,
For better or worse,
You'll understand something.
Ignorance, is stupidity,
Arrogance, self gloating conceition.
Inability of adaptability,
The desire of control,
Of surroundings,
For emotional stability.
These are ignorances,
Beyond frustrating,
And gestures of real,
Negativity.
A messy headache,
And non,
But bullshit.

ANGER

It's perfectly okay to be fucking angry.
IT'S PERFECTLY OKAY TO BE FUCKING ANGRY!!!!!
But be careful about what spite smites.
Think about what crosses the bridge,
Before you go and burn down the villages.
There isn't always the need of conflict or to pillage.
Delegations signed by blood say to fucking end this.
Often times a show of self awareness,
And unethical projections withholding dormant.
Don't let a river of magma stay constant,
Or like Yellowstone waiting to explode.
Learn to channel the way that the spirit flows.
Damage nothing but always burning,
The coldest, brightest, warmest, flame.

Topiaries

Point place,
Roundabouts town,
Unrest can't find a moment,
To relax and calm down,
Unless asleep and sound.
Hostilities can't let guard down,
In collection of irritants and frowns,
Disappointed joke of clowns.
Another failed approach,
The dance of the cockroach.
No sense, making cents,
To prove worthiness,
In false existence,
Of fabricated living.

Glasswares

A cup not yet filled with its' fun,
Never full, and never enough.
An exchange you must offer up,
Cut yourself, bleeding upon all.
Blood as sacrifice, wares of spite,
The opened wound draws the line.
Everything sharpened,
Bladed edged,
To bowls of rice,
The chairs and tables,
Plates and utensils handles.
Damage unavoidable,
Anything you touch,
Bizarre shoppe.
Filleting your flesh,
The force of life,
Draining from your chest.
Pools down the grooves,
Guiding the floor,
All for personal entertainment.
Goreful afflictions,
Painful anguish,
To someone elses benefit,
An alchemical experiment.

Signal Towers

Feels like forced affection,
A weak connection,
And…
The signal is lost…
To wilderness, gone,
Hidden in its' rediscovery.
Knowledge of the ancients,
Counsel of the spirits.
Prehistoric texts of long ago,
To be remembered,
Not kept,
To have learned,
Not forgetting.
An act of letting go,
To rise with the glowing orb,
And see beyond,
The futures of the road.

Born of Death

Yeah, yeah, yeah,
This seems to be the spot.
Hand over the athame,
I've brought the black magic box.
Take and pierce the throat,
Of blinded innocence.
Twisted in crimson water flow,
The shrieks of the waterfalls.
The struggle and gurgle,
Both forced, beaten to a point,
Fear taken will and choice,
To quiet a poor boy.
They already sold,
Their ruinous soul.
All for trade,
Shards of crystals,
And fools gold.
They wanted mine to trade,
I refused,
Still, they did anyways.
Leaving a cold dream waking,
And a repeated shiver quaking.

The Tormentor

Dark forces and evil lurk,
Real, and torturous cruelty,
Unforgivable tormentation,
Nightmaric fascinations,
Insomniatic awakenings.
The strangler of strangers,
At midnight terrors,
The tormentor.
Weak, pitiful,
Putrid, vile,
And balding.
A weak link of blood,
Powerless against all.
A destructive sadist,
Who's strength comes,
Of nothingness and meanness.
Equivalence of garbage.

Cure

Purify the heart,
Somehow, someway.
Cut it out,
In preparation,
For spiritual surgery.
Salt it,
Frankenstien replacement,
Of robotic cybernetics.
Must be cleaned proper,
In a divine cure.

The Viciousness of Wind

Uprooting the trees effortlessly,
Splitting the mountains in two pieces.
The movement of water,
Be it of ocean or river,
The wind will deliver.
Hushing the snowy valleys,
Or at blazed laughter,
In clanking clamoring chatter.
To turn of joys,
Stiff and frigid.
A callous reminder of remainders,
Severance of heirs and retainers.
Disturbed airs vent in trace of despair,
It's presence passing by,
Something heartfelt,
But never held.

Gossip

Filters idealized and defined,
Perceptively selfish and unrefined,
By the state and shape of mind.
Formed impeded by eyes,
Only words to describe,
From their essence of life.
Brain dead but so very alive,
In the moment of present time.
As sandy ashes, crumble to the ground,
Only ghost of whispers die down.

Poinsettia

Poinsettia of Snows,
Delicate bristles,
Endearing,
As they are fragile,
And so gentle.
Rarity poised in elegance,
Mosaics' bloom of a lifetime.
With bloodied hands,
To still have plucked,
The flowers.

Ashen Dance

From origin of embers.
More than the rains,
Entering my mind,
Visitors of time.
The world stopped,
In orbit forgot,
The day bore of no wrongness.
Pink divide, of dollhouse sight,
Following along into the night.
The beauty of moonlight,
The mystics ancient,
Mossend cloak,
Synergized magics.
Star gems a decorative,
Compliment garnishing,
Fit for a fine Goddess!
Stimulate and articulate,
The expansion of conscience.
As one at soul,
Tethered by love,
The promise of romantics.

Animal Abuse

Froze paralytically within death,
Aquaria crevices only in brokenness.
No resuscitation or resurrection,
Stiff in dilections.
Undeserving of love, trust and affections.
Fearful to foul reactions,
Tormented and beaten with cruelty.
Source of infinite loyalty,
Limited time exchanged,
Far from luxuries,
In limb discovery.
Sadly put through suffering,
For pathetic reasons of nothing.
A cup for misery,
And unsettling reality disturbing.
Bullied to death so disgustingly.
Eyes rolled on back,
A haunting burnt to memory,
And existence gone in an instance.
Fucked up.
Rocco.

Sacredness of Tears

Isolate until you feel safe,
Enough to break.
Harvest hour, before sorrowful sows,
Where it pours down the rain.
Around the heart collecting,
It's aura rejuvenating.
Tears wept,
You know you can't reject,
A wound when it's there.
Acknowledge and tend to it,
Without a boastful ignorance,
And you will begin to see,
Difference within indifference.

The Flag

An allegiance of my youth,
Symbolic flag.
We swore an oath,
For thirteen years.
Some 'weird occult type shit.'

Arguments

Both of pointed truth,
Acknowledgements justifiable,
Yet a conflict is still a brew.
People just like to bitch and argue.
One of fallacies,
One that's factually,
Fire just barking up the fuse.
People just like to bitch and argue.
Idiots,
Either incomplete,
Utter incompetence,
Idealized, but far from truths.
Passionate but in bicker none knew.
People just like to bitch and argue.

The Haunted Laptop

I didn't fuck with the pad I swear.
Toggle on fritz,
Mouse in a blitz,
Fucking Feddy OP did this?
A ghost,
Or fucking computer glitch?
Off and on,
Widgets and fidgets.
Porn of the midgets,
Is it,
Is it a virus?
Ascend the coding of digits,
And please fix this.

The World Librarium

Each person its own,
Genrenized book.
Each sliver a written bit,
Of conscious being.
Speak any page,
By glance of look.
History left to dusty,
Old shelves,
Ancient knowledge,
Still to be discovered.
Of the seen,
And the felt,
Mysterious,
Whereabouts.
Brought from the whispers of the dead,
And of the livings breath.
Conversations,
And fullness to recover.
The World Librarium,
The very experience,
Of all that makes up you.

Can of Energy

Can of energy,
Potion of electricity.
A poisoned water substitute,
But healthier than amphetamine.
Would probably kill the ancestors,
Anatomically probably couldn't handle it,
Overloaded, the heart would blow apart.

Alchemical Substances

Lang ago,
Before 1955,
Somebody couldn't handle their high.
The narc freaked and illegalized,
Things already out of their control.
Substrate to frustrate,
And baseless claims,
Other than fear that takes place.
Ultra mass study hypnotic,
The law of self,
Convincing you,
To disobey.
Who are you anyways.
The paper tasteless.
The derangement extends through,
The experiment convinces you.
Of brewery and potions,
Pharmacological extortions,
The naturalist devotion.
Getting high is perfectly alright,
Understanding a balance in life,
And science of effects.
Will and choice,
Are of one volition,
And journeys out,

Upon new found missions.
Universal and unreligious.
An experience,
Shared as human.

Reason

Repeated renditions,
Side quest repetitions.
To acquire new skills,
Sailing upon the main quested.
Of dreams lively and not at rest.
At tour of artful request,
As the renascence,
Continued sequence.
Pillagment of documented history,
Fulfillment of violence,
Dawning of the freeing,
Perceptual senses.
Beyond reason,
And senses,
The consensus of,
Philosophical resentments.
Inflective influensive theoreticals,
Keep it all personal,
Disregarding of all incentives,
And of modernistic mimics.
The gambit of ambition,
And only words left to say.
Here I am to leave a stain,
For you to interpret.
I've come here,

To carve a piece of myself,
Onto the throne of hell.
To all that follow,
Well, I do,
Wish you well.

Care

An ambience of movement,
Background dwellings,
Curiosities in exploring.
Left the graveyard,
Early this morning.
To tend and care,
To those still living.
Shepard overbearing,
To love and protect,
With powers,
Bestowed from death.
The one whom walks forever,
Observer of silence,
Knots tying,
As the rest of time.
Begins unwinding.

Fillet Human

Another piece of meat,
Doth step to seek,
Seems they want to feel and bleed,
They brought the wrong kind of beef.

THICC

Ooey, gooey,
Thick and moist,
A softness, a craving,
Delicasse' choice, the obvious.
That which plus and gravitates,
Magical jiggles, bounce and wiggles.
Astonishing motions oscillate,
Blessing those befalling pathway.
Punctuate pulsation,
Between organ, soul, and sensation.
Blushed sightly in adoration.
To lay my face,
Upon such beauty,
From beyond greatest imaginations.
The most cushiony of pillows.

Cerebral:
Darwinistic Trauma Theory

A triggered pulled,
Activating hidden mechanisms,
Quite stately and dissociative.
The brain consciously sentient,
Draws away in neural deactivation.
Instigated awareness,
Signaling detection,
In mental mediation.
Information pools and gathers,
Processing the psyches survival of reality.
In preservation of the mind,
And energy of self sustainability.
Learning strange and unique abilities,
Such as some form of energetic invisibility,
Where life force cannot empathically be felt,
Or even sensed, remaining undetected.
Eyes known to pierce through silence,
And ears that see the source.
The mystery of the brain, misinterpreted,
Misinformed, organically limiting its' full force .
Does more than I'll know,
With knowledge never to show,
Putting to actions,
What's widely disregarded and unknown.

Such powers shrouded undeciphered,
Right next to those micro plastic fibers.
Traumatized through the years,
To the day by day of current hours.
With much there is to disagree,
Deeper than disorder,
Simpler than illness,
Created within circumstances.
With the brain as your witness,
A small piece of creation,
Developing into its norm,
Finding peace of understandings,
A novelty of modern evolution.

Just be as is,
Truly to life's testament.

Duplicates

Summonings of eternal grey,
Find their way through rusted drains,
Rains, barred up the windows,
And busting out the glass.
Paints all around stained,
Next to such artful remains.
Mind pollution douchery,
Take the image,
Copied and pasted.
Fearing of true debauchery,
Dreams all shattered,
Broken up on the ground,
For their children to gather.
Lost all together,
Crisis in initiation,
How does the theatre look?
None is real,
All is staged,
The Societal Play.
A gamble fronted game,
Masking and sealing away,
The best parts of human ways.
How do you actually feel?

Mind Rot

Sporadic happenings,
Irritations and irrational mess,
Who's left to clean up the fucking spill.
Be it too much,
Or too little,
Is all that's left to feel.
Away with compromises,
Nothingness left in place,
All else sapped and taken.
Up early and late,
To be as one,
Elevate a mental state,
Clawing at some sense of peace,
Before I get checked into State.
So much at once,
Can't catch a break,
Bake bread, sell or trade,
In the end,
Alone to frustrate.
At waste with plastics so fake,
Misunderstandings,
Only fuel conflicts and rage.
A cast of confusion and hate,
Keeps vibrancies displaced.
The only constitute of truth,

And resolute ambition thats true.
With pain and misery all around you,
Joy is the worthy,
And most bountiful construit.

Entrapped

Each blemish around,
Is a trap,
Of someones personal,
Checking account.
To contract thee,
Of all amenities,
Taxing all basis,
Rent to groceries.
Entrapment guised as opportunity.
Schooling to hire workers,
Instead of those free thinkers,
Or those undermined as tinkers.
At numerical value of society,
Replacing volunteering slaves,
Image falsely as community,
Egotistically they skirmish for supplies,
But much to their surprise they'll still die.
Instead of together to strive,
Someone thought themselves,
So much better.

Current of Pangea

Gaianic puzzlement,
Dethroning of Pangea,
The worlds once known,
Drifting, breaking apart.
Wonderment cast to abandonment,
Captured and enfrenzied,
Confined much like a genie.
Crossing lines much imaginary,
Killed in another country,
Invader of foreign bodies.
Finding yourself amidst commotion,
On a planet irrationilzed by Nation.

—

A white supremacist,
Gets fucked by a black guy.
Enough said.
Poetic homosexuality.

—

Wake of Birds

At new slate of mind,
Letting go of things,
Meant to pass with time.
Slaying the way it was,
Mystics to change,
And the ceremony starts, and begins.
Lighting of sage and incense,
At home in the jungles,
Offerings of flesh and smoke,
To walk the natural sense,
Ethereals of nonbeing.
A summoning we seek,
In the forests heart,
A deep sleep.
Reawakening of Dawn,
The birds as alarms,
Feathers and dreams,
Shake from branches and trees,
Within the reclamations of spirit.
Solitudes resonance of independence,
Alone company to enjoy the silences,
A blaze with fires exhibitions,
That taunts upon the fermentation.

Reptilians

A reptilian to heat,
Can't move so lazily.
On a rock a bit too comfortable.
The warmth of the sun is bliss,
Soak and absorb all of this.
A terrarium, cave artificium,
Created habitats,
Adapting the environment,
To sensual desires.
The curse against natures anguish.

First Spill

First bloods drawn,
Binding something demonic.
Manifested physical pneumonic,
Warped and wicked,
Fighting farce,
The stars aligned at fate,
And the blade had a little taste.
A youthful lesson of stabbing,
Grade six goblenic.
Ancient and chaotic,
The daemon a prisoner,
Within the shell of vessel.
A difference starved and begging.
Unexpected ominous,
Acquainted year long hauntings.
Combative sadisticals,
Didn't hesitate at impulse,
Left a hole gushing out,
Under the stairwell,
All quieted down.
Screaming and crying aloud,
Into the shadows,
Our pathway out.

The Bunker

We've hunkered down,
Defending the bunker.
In maintenance of a money bog,
Up and down it's spirit creaks,
Emptied rooms hollowed by ingratitude.
Cave waters toxified by poisonous retirement,
The pesticides leave no compromise,
Leaving you bitterness to spit and foulness of attitude.
Maintenance of survival, failure of establishings.
Unrest and at sacrifice, all at blight,
Over time its defense broken-down,
Eroding into the parables of light.
Warm or cold the constant strife,
Windows cracked and then some foil,
Arms in passing by, locked down.
Boxes to prepare for the summons,
Of a new place of order.
Down to two, a fuzzied beast.
All thats left in remnants,
The bunker within the settlement of the city.
Remains of purging and change,
Seeded wisdom through darken pain,
It was by tree that he'd invade.
The suffrage of growth,
And bullet holes pave,

In ricochet of waves,
All to have willfully known.
By our efforts, and what we've chose,
But no choice within our plunder,
To abandon post, leaving the bunker.
In meditation, and transmuting matter,
Repositioning where the sunlight scatters.

The Alter of Humanity

At long, long halls,
We breathe and eat,
And for one nights sake,
Out the cold to take our peace.
Looking into the deepest,
Specture of souls,
Spectrum each its' own.
Fractally congregated,
Surrounded by joys of soup,
With ghosts now long gone.
Leaving new life space,
Freely to grow into,
A shapeless mold.

Secret Art:
Shibari

Creations Masterpiece,
A personal blessing,
In ritualistic setting,
You are mine,
And I'm not sharing.
Quiver to touch of skin,
Bounding ourselves,
Together again.
Sadistic chivalry,
Dark and gently.
Your heart is all I need,
The only thing that can appease,
Endearingly, your body,
I seek to please.
Ranged roulette,
Of emotional sensitivity,
Playfully sexually.
Tying up my precious gift,
The universe had sent me,
Ever so respectfully.
I've finished fastening the rope,
And now there is nowhere left to go.

Nursery

Homie got snatched up,
In the middle of his shift.
Another strangers nose,
Is where the narcan goes,
Who would of guessed it.
His people dipped,
And left him for dead.
Competing with Sisyphus,
Greeting occupants of syphilis,
And presume ideals chrysalis.
A grown man whines and bitches,
Again and again,
Arguments, dismiss them.
I don't want to fucking listen,
I already have two ears full.
Glass bouncing from the floor,
New goons walk thru the door.
Judgment is empty,
Filling the void of nothingness,
Instead of conclusively understanding.
The mushrooms,
Aren't some secret power up,
To enhance intelligence,
You're just high an opinionated.
By the final straw of simplicity,

Parting words, to drop and quit,
  Another number rotating out.

The Medicine of Sleep

A much need cure,
For an insomniac,
Too afraid to dream.
Hauntingly to sleep,
Slumber lullabies,
Slip away, to hibernate.
To heal some wound keeping me awake,
Surgeance of contemplation,
By the thoughts,
Obliterations.
Self destruction,
Reliving heartbreak,
And its devastations.
The kindled echo,
Gone cold,
Left the flame frozen.
To begin again,
After the dying Winters,
Relighting its flicker.
The Medicine of Sleep,
The cabinets are empty,
So today, I'll step back,
And refresh in this delight.

Strawberry Kisses

Jealousy an awful confession,
Mixed with madness,
And long term,
Derangement.
Existential confusion,
Excuse anothers,
Illusions in profusion,
Convincingly proven.
Smoke signals,
The only way,
To communicate.
Disintegrated,
By ideas delicious.
A lesbians,
Strawberry Kisses,
A misunderstanding,
Painfully of consequence.
New pajamas began to lit,
Long fused overreactions,
Psychotic implosions.
I slept in the other room,
And kicked right the fuck out.
Dimethyltryptamine woods,
Exploring an outcome for good.
To stand firm and true,

Into the calmness of brew.
The enchantment has broken,
New light shines upon truth,
Jammed up on, strawberry kisses.
In absence of preceding presents,
Trust is the viable pretense left,
Standing.

Rustic Decay

Old buildings and dismantled machines,
Urbanization falling to nature.
The weeper rains,
Of short walked roads.
By end of old human ways,
What day remains left to reclaim,
Those moments past,
Here they are to waste.

Macrooned

Eviscerating
Tastes buds,
At touch of taste,
That bursts upon your face.
Vitality coming back again,
In form of nucleic explosions!
A dozen devoured,
And the box went missing.
What maybe, be it,
Gem, biscuit or cookie?
A little creme in the nookies.

—

A stone sinks,
Drowning in the sands,
Becoming one,
Eroding away,
To earthened seas.

—

A Call To Adventure

Songs and note chasing the very winds,
A call to adventure,
A call to adventure.
Through forest dew, and weaving rivers,
A call to adventure,
A call to adventure.

Alive in the flames,
Burning by day,
True to our wildest ways.
Fanning flute,
'Ol tune the satyr plays.
In harmony,
Of slaughtering screams,
Change discovered,
Each passing scene.
Explorer imagine,
Everything yet to see,
Sanctuaries mystique,
Hidden in silence.
Lost to nature.

Molted leaves cloak mountainous stairs,
A call to adventure,
A call to adventure.

Over parched desert and deaths snare,
A call to adventure,
A call to adventure.

Alive in the flames,
Burning by day,
True to our wildest ways.
Fanning flute,
'Ol tune the satyr plays.
In harmony,
Of slaughtering screams,
Change discovered,
Each passing scene.
Explorer imagine,
Everything yet to see,
Sanctuaries mystique,
Hidden in silence.
Lost to nature.

A call to adventure,
A call to adventure.

Abandon Thy Name

Abandon thy name,
Spilling thy wisdom,
Peeling layers of shame,
Shedding all that you do fear.

Dried plains veiling thunder,
Scorched arena battle grounds.
Evasion invitation to succumber,
The leafless barren escapades.
Hunt, don't prey upon pity.

Abandon thy name,
Spilling thy wisdom,
Peeling layers of shame,
Shedding all that you do fear.

No doubt crossing vast oceans,
Instincts sharpened,
No trembling emotions.
Limber up cause and reaction,
Pouncing freely from faction.

Rebelling against gods and devils alike.

Abandon thy name,

Spilling thy wisdom,
Peeling layers of shame,
Shedding all that you do fear.

Fiery maned,
Untamed,
They are,
The lions.

Gamble of Heart

Guest statues filling rooms with chatter,
Luxuries fine hour in hallway laughter.

Do you trust and do you know,
Rolling dice in the casino.
Your spirit does linger,
Toss a ring on your finger.
Never at loss or regret of lost cards.

Will hearts align?
Cherish chance of time,
No roulette charade; the risks apparent,
What'll it be...?
Loves a gamble of heart my lady,
Who's the winner of the lottery?

Midas touch, Medusa's gold,
Reaping harvest treasure troves,
Cashing out fine jewels and stones,
To give you my all,
Without the hope of return.

Will hearts align?
Cherish chance of time,
No roulette charade; the risks apparent,

What'll it be...?
Loves a gamble of heart my lady,
Who's the winner of the lottery?

Travel to the centered soul,
Weight dropped from the edge of worlds.
Mirrors scry truth beyond deepening eyes,
Quality assured, won't you join my side?
A distant cold heart finds,
You've been missing out of my time.

Poetress of ancient dreams, touched so personally,
Peasants love of royalty, guides the goddess to
eternity,
Setting souls where the sunrise seeks a final moments
peace,
Together revel locked arms rejoice the hour we greet.

Will hearts align?
Cherish chance of time,
No roulette charade; the risks apparent,
What'll it be...?
Loves a gamble of heart my lady,
Who's the winner of the lottery?
I feel its' me!

Full Course Meal

[Seatting]
Palette just for taste,
I'll finish every bite on my plate.
Lick it clean, a full course meal,
Fine dining and cutlery steel.
I'm gonna eat you baby!

[Hors D'ouvres]
Tease, tormenting, tongue tantalizing,
Taking to the tenderlands,
Soft and tender breads,
Bake beneath the heat.
Tease, uhuh, entree appease,
This is just the beginning of the feast!

[Meat Dish/Fish]
Foams expanding celibacy,
Creeping slowly to the shore.
Oh, mystic creature of the deep,
To please with gratitude and appreciation.
Oh mermaid, no sands cursing my eyes,
Soul of all hidden treasures,
Conversion tips the scales,
Of time and pleasure.

[Maincourse]
Applaud and shout about!
Release a primal growl!
Bound, and cast down,
Chained and roped,
Took the time to smoke.
Getting hot now,
Even better seared,
Dark desires enflamed,.
Oh succubus awake,
Great demoness of lust!
Rare meats to taste buds,
In ritualistic offerings.

[Salad]
Sensually,
The fresh forest vegetation,
Anchor to the earths.
Toss and churn.
A salad mixture,
Toss and churn.
Let chemistry work,
It's sexual spiritual force.
Vines drop begging the dew soaked soils,
As the sun takes a dip, setting into the sea.

[Cheese]
Let me see that coffee stained smile again,
Brightly coy grin of joy,

Know how to make a man from a boy.
Delicacy light it sees,
By the very graces of Aphrodite.

[Dessert]
Oooh, it's here, it's here,
The dessert is here.

Goddamn look at that cake!
Squishy pillow fun to spank,
Taking just a piece, a sure mistake,
Bring it all, the goddamn cake!
Put it down right on my plate!

[Drink]
Cloaked in silky nakedness,
Depleted strength spills.
Cuddled sleepily in arms of rest,
Rejuvenating embrace and warm caress,
The way your head lays on my chest.
The time for lovers to feel refreshed.

But I still hunger,
For a Full Course Meal.

Pompei

This ones a disturbance in nature.
Twisting whirls gusts of flame,
Opening hell's pits, infernal heatwave,
Wrath of hatred's rage,
Wrath of hatred's rage.

And there it goes,
Pompei explodes!
Boiling the seas,
Setting fires,
To the hairs of the trees.
Magma flooding armageddon,
Another martyr of destruction.
And there it goes,
Pompei explodes!

Won't let this burn die in vain,
Fueling the wildfires flame,
Singed, cinders, of pain,
Wrath of hatred's rage,
Wrath of hatred's rage!

And there it goes,
Pompei explodes!
Boiling the seas,

Setting fires,
To the hairs of the trees.
Magma flooding armageddon,
Another martyr of destruction.
And there it goes,
Pompei explodes!

Lifeline Soul Bindment:
Black Magic Spell

Putting everything on the line,
Even trading your own life,
The most precious of gifts and decide.

To the soul in bounds, linked alive,
A dark contract, the one true birth right,
And if betrayed only death awaits.
The spell casters only fate;
If failure to dedicate,
To the very nature,
Of ones own way.

I Shall not fail, nor fall,
Material will never be a wall.
I shall not give up, nor run,
To lose all of my blood, and still overcome.
I shall not show cowardice, nor fear,
Except to those of importance, and hold dear.
I shall not falter, nor abandon,
In honor of choice and all ambitions.
I shall not lose, nor be defeated,
Prevailing against foeful spirits of the world.

Here now manifesting,

Against even the tides of fate itself.
Through any and all means,
Beyond aeons of divine happenings.
Here now manifesting,
The drive of individual fires,
Passionate lone magic acquired,
From there all that you could desire.
Here now manifesting,
From this moment a change in all things,
Dreams drip from the mind into reality,
From sharpened will and mentality.
Here now manifesting,
Summoning to the physicality of the realm,
Portals opening from the current of soul,
Surfacing upon the shape of the world.
Here now manifesting,
Bleeding into existence the unseen now born,
Abidements of thoughts, feeling, and energies stored,
By the only source the spirits human core.
Here now manifesting,
Directly from the life force,
All pressure from me in omission,
Freely released in spiritual exertion.

Oi, that's it,
You've made it to the end.
Good for you,
Reading and all that.
Do it again,
It's healthy.
But until then,
The Djinn has finished,
His fine bottle of Gin.